Table of Contents

Introduction

1. Pork Vegetable Hotpot

2. Thai Vegetable Beef Hotpot

3. Spicy Noodle Hotpot

4. Thai Beef Hotpot

5. Thai Lemongrass Hotpot

6. Thai curry noodles soup

7. Lamb Hotpot

8. Thai Lamb Hotpot

9. Beef Noodle Soup

10. Lamb Noodle Hotpot Soup

11. Thai Shrimp Hotpot

12. Egg Noodle Hotpot

13. Ramen Shrimp Hotpot

14. Prawn and Noodle Hotpot

15. Chicken Noodle Soup

16. Duck Noodle Soup

17. Ramen Chicken Hotpot

18. Chicken Ramen Soup

19. Spicy Beef and Mushroom Stew

20. Lamb Pea Soup

21. Tofu Pea Soup

[22. Beef Ramen Soup with Veggies](#)

[23. Cauliflower Pea Soup](#)

[24. Chicken Lemongrass Soup](#)

[25. Mushroom Soup](#)

[26. Thai Mushroom Hotpot](#)

[27. Chicken Curry Udon Hotpot](#)

[28. Penang laksa](#)

[29. Japanese Veggie Curry](#)

[30. Tofu Lemongrass Soup](#)

[Conclusion](#)

[Author's Afterthoughts](#)

Introduction

Looking for ways to use that Hotpot of yours at home? If so, you're in the right place. This book contains a variety of Hotpot recipes that can be made by even the most beginner cook! This book contains recipes that are soupy and broth-filled and which allows your guests to do some partial cooking in the Hotpot.

Almost all the recipes here are easy and beginner-friendly. With basic ingredients and detailed instructions, you and your guests will be enjoying your Hotpot in no time! Let's begin!

1. Pork Vegetable Hotpot

Looking for a healthy meal to serve that is also tasty? Then, this Hotpot recipe could be the answer. This dish is filled with nutritious pork, vegetables, and spices.

Time: 55 minutes

Serves: 2-3

Ingredients:

- 3 carrots
- 1 cup green beans
- 4 green onions
- chili sauce (as desired)
- hot pepper sauce (as desired)
- 1 pkg thin Rice noodles
- 1 tbsp olive oil
- 1 cup mushrooms
- 3 cups vegetable stock

- 4 tbsp soy sauce, low-sodium
- Lean, thinly sliced
- Ginger

Directions:

Grate the ginger and slice the mushrooms. Cut the green beans then slice the carrots thinly. Cut the green onions and set aside.

Cook rice noodles according to package instructions.

Set a large saucepan over medium heat then add some oil to the pan. Once the oil in the pan is slightly heated, add the mushrooms and allow them to cook for about 3 minutes.

Add the soy sauce, ginger, stock, and chili sauce. Mix all the ingredients into a pan and bring to a boil.

Add the carrots, green beans, and green onions then allow them to cook.

Transfer broth into Hotpot and set it onto the burner on your table.

Transfer the noodles to individual serving bowls and add stock. Allow the guests to dip pork into Hotpot to cook and enjoy the veggies and noodles. Have a few dipping sauces on the table as well. Enjoy

2. Thai Vegetable Beef Hotpot

This is an enjoyable Hotpot recipe that is also comforting and filling. The broth has a sweet and savory flavor, primarily if you use mirin, which is naturally sweet. You will undoubtedly enjoy the tofu and all the different veggies, too.

Time: 40 mins

Servings: 8

Ingredients:

Boiling water

- 1 lb. tender beef, well-marbled, sliced extra thinly
- 5 scallions, green and white parts only, 2" lengths diagonally
- 9 oz tofu, firm, cubed
- 2 carrots, peeled, diagonally cut
- 2 celery stalks, diagonally cut
- 1 onion, halved, yellow
- 1 cup mushrooms, fresh, chopped

- Bottled dipping sauce of your choice

Directions:

Soak noodles into an oven-safe bowl for approximately 3 minutes in boiling water.

Carefully, drain your noodles, then rinse them under cold water. Slice noodles in half.

In a large pot, heat the beef stock and oil over medium-high heat. Add the mushrooms, celery, carrots, green onions, and yellow onion. Stir while cooking for about 5 minutes.

Transfer broth to the Hotpot that is over the burner on the table. Set the individual bowls for your guests then ladle broth into them. Have fondue forks or chopsticks ready for your guests to use to dip their meat into the broth and sauces. Add noodles to the broth.

Have dipping sauce on the table and enjoy!

3. Spicy Noodle Hotpot

This is a quick soup recipe, but don't let that fool you. It is very satisfying. It provides a spicy flavor, in addition to cilantro, lime, ginger and soy sauce. Some of the spices will be too hot for young children, but you can just leave out some of the spicier ingredients in the children's Hotpot.

Time: 45 mins

Servings: 6

Ingredients:

- 3/4 lb. ribeye beef, boneless, sliced thinly
- 3/4 lb. large shrimp, deveined, peeled
- 1×2" piece ginger, peeled and sliced
- ½ head 2''Napa cabbage, top leaves and stem pieces separated
- 4 oz shiitake, stemmed, thinly sliced
- 1 (32 oz) Container of beef broth
- 2 tbsp brown sugar

- 2 tbsp chili paste
- 3 tbsp vegetable oil
- 1/4 cup Cilantro, chopped
- 8 oz fettuccine pasta
- 2 tbsp toasted sesame oil
- 3 tbsp low-sodium soy sauce

Directions:

Heat vegetable oil into a saucepan over medium-high heat. Add the ginger and stir while cooking for about a minute.

Add mushrooms and occasionally stir while cooking until they are soft. About 2 to 3 minutes.

Add the brown sugar and chili paste occasionally stirring while cooking for ½ a minute.

Add the chicken broth, 1 cup water, and soy sauce. Add cabbage and bring to a boil. Lower the heat of your broth and allow it to simmer for 25 minutes.

In a large pot, add the salted boiling water. Cook the pasta according to package directions. Drain pasta and rinse under cool, then cold water. Toss with 1 tablespoon of sesame oil.

Stir the leaves of cabbage into the broth. Bring broth to a boil. Add 1 tablespoon of sesame oil and cilantro.

Divide noodles among the serving bowls and add the hot broth and veggies.

Place the thinly sliced meat onto a platter on the table. Allow your guests to cook slices as they prefer. Enjoy.

4. Thai Beef Hotpot

This Hotpot recipe is a variation on a broader Asian Hotpot medley. It begins with a rich stock that is spiced with garlic, ginger and curry paste. Your guests are sure to enjoy scooping broth and noodles into their serving bowls, while they quickly cook their meat in the stock.

Time: 30 mins

Servings: 10

Ingredients:

- 2 tbsp fresh lime juice
- 1 tbsp garlic powder
- 1 tsp ground ginger
- 2 tbsp low sodium soy sauce
- 1 tbsp brown sugar, lightly packed
- 2 tsp vegetable oil

- 1 sweet onion, thinly sliced, large
- 2 (32 oz) containers of beef stock
- 1/4 cup, red curry paste

Protein:

- 1 lb. Flank steak, thinly sliced

Sauces

- Tangy chili sauce
- Dipping sauce that you desire
- Cooked Lo Mein Noodles

Directions:

To create a broth, heat the oil into a large stock pot on med-high heat. Add the onion then stir to combine, cook until tender.

Keep stirring while you add garlic powder, soy sauce, ginger, curry past, brown sugar, and stock. Bring to a boil then lower heat. Cover pan. Simmer for 20 minutes before adding lime juice into the broth.

Place the thinly sliced steak onto a plate then add garnishes into bowls. Place your choice of dipping sauce on the table.

Pour broth into your Hotpot on the table, over a burner. Allow your guests to cook their steak slices in the broth for a few minutes.

Your guests can customize their individual serving bowls with sauces, garnishes, etc. Place the cooked Lo Mein noodles in their bowls and ladle broth over the noodles. Enjoy.

5. Thai Lemongrass Hotpot

This recipe is a great Hotpot recipe for entertaining. Your guests will do most of the cooking! It is flexible, so you can make it appeal to everyone. Your guests are sure to have a good time while they enjoy this healthy, hearty meal!

Time: 25 mins

Servings: 8-10

Ingredients:

- 1 head, Napa cabbage
- 2 heads broccoli
- 1 large bok choy
- 1 tbsp granulated sugar
- 2 tsp fish sauce
- 1 tsp paprika
- 1 tsp salt
- 4 cloves garlic, minced

- 5 red chilies, dried
- 3 tbsp lemongrass, minced
- 2 shallots
- 1 3''ginger
- 1 onion, sliced
- 12 cups, chicken broth
- 6 stalks lemongrass
- 8 oz mushrooms, sliced
- 6 leaves Kaffir lime

Protein:
- 1 lb. beef, the eye of round
- 1 lb. shrimp, deveined, peeled

Directions:

Smash the roots of your lemongrass stalks, then toss them into a large stockpot.

Slice your piece of ginger lengthwise in half then peel the skin. Peel your onion and cut it into halves then add to the stockpot.

Add 8 cups of broth to stockpot then bring mixture to a boil and set on simmer. Simmer pot over medium-low for about one hour.

As the broth simmers, mince your shallots and garlic finely.

Heat 3 tbsp. of oil then add the lemongrass, garlic, shallots. Cook for a few minutes until the garlic begins to turn golden in color. Remove the pan from heat. Add the red chilies and paprika. Combine by stirring. This will be one of your dipping sauces.

Add Sugar along with 1 teaspoon of salt to the broth, along with the lime leaves. Adjust the taste of the broth using the fish sauce if you desire. The broth is now ready.

Thinly slice the meat and veggies and place on plates.

Add the remainder of the chicken broth to the broth mixture, along with mushrooms and stir well. Add 2 to 3 tablespoons of sauce made in step 5 and adjust the taste as you like.

Add the broth to the Hotpot on the table, over the burner.

Set the meat and veggies plates out, along with fondue forks or chopsticks.

Ladle broth into individual serving bowls and allow your guests to cook their veggies and meats as they like. Enjoy.

6. Thai curry noodles soup

The Thai restaurant around the corner has nothing on you. Learn how to prepare this awesome soup and never have to eat out again (unless you are going for something else then soup, of course)

Time: 50 mins

Servings: 4

Ingredients:

- 1 tbsp. sesame oil
- 2 green onions, minced
- 1 tbsp garlic, minced
- 1 large carrot, peeled and grated
- 1 tbsp lemongrass, minced
- 1 tbsp fresh ginger, minced
- 6 cups turkey broth
- 2 tbsp yellow or orange curry paste

- ½ cup uncooked white rice
- ¼ cup fresh chopped parsley, cilantro mixture
- 1 can light coconut milk
- 1 tbsp lime juice
- Salt, black pepper

Directions:

Heat oil in a skillet cook the garlic, lemongrass, mixed fresh herbs, ginger, green onions and carrots for about 10 minutes or so. Set aside.

In a pot, bring to boil coconut milk mixed with the turkey broth.

Add the curry paste, coconut milk, lime juice and all other spices.

Use a whisk and stir until the curry has dissolved and then add the uncooked rice.

Bring them the temperature to medium-low and continue cooking until rice is cooked.

Serve with your favorite crackers.

7. Lamb Hotpot

A delicious lamb Hotpot recipe with rice noodles and veggies.

Time: 55 minutes

Serves: 2-3

Ingredients:

- 3 carrots
- 1 cup green beans
- 4 green onions
- Chili sauce (as desired)
- Hot pepper sauce (as desired)
- 1 pkg thin Rice noodles
- 1 tbsp olive oil
- 1 cup mushrooms
- 3 cups vegetable stock
- 4 tbsp low-sodium soy sauce
- Lean Lamb, thinly sliced
- Ginger

Directions:

Grate the ginger and slice the mushrooms. Cut the green beans then slice the carrots thinly. Cut the green onions and set aside.

Cook rice noodles according to package instructions.

Set a large saucepan over medium heat then add some oil to the pan. Once the oil in the pan is slightly heated, add the mushrooms and allow them to cook for about 3 minutes.

Add the soy sauce, ginger, stock, and chili sauce. Mix all the ingredients into a pan and bring to a boil.

Add the carrots, green beans, and green onions then allow them to cook.

Transfer broth into Hotpot and set it onto the burner on your table.

Transfer the noodles to serving bowls add stock. Allow the guests to dip lamb into Hotpot to cook and enjoy the veggies and noodles. Have a few dipping sauces on the table as well. Enjoy!

8. Thai Lamb Hotpot

A delicious Hotpot experience with lamb and Thai spices.

Time: 30 mins

Servings: 10

Ingredients:

- 2 tbsp fresh Lime juice
- 1 tbsp garlic powder
- 1 tsp ground ginger
- 2 tbsp low sodium soy sauce
- 1 tbsp brown sugar, lightly packed
- 2 tsp vegetable oil
- 1 large sweet onion, thinly sliced
- 2 (32 oz) Containers of beef stock
- 1/4 cup red curry paste

Protein:
- 1 lb. lamb flank, thinly sliced

Sauces
- Tangy chili sauce
- Dipping sauce that you desire
- Cooked Lo Mein Noodles

Directions:

To create a broth, heat the oil into a large stockpot over medium-high heat. Add the onion, then stir to combine, cook until tender.

Stir while you add garlic powder, ginger, soy sauce, brown sugar, curry paste, and stock. Bring to boil then lower heat. Cover pan. Simmer for 20 mins then mix in the lime juice into the broth.

Place the thinly sliced steak onto a plate then add garnishes into bowls. Place your choice of dipping sauce on the table.

Pour broth into your Hotpot on the table, over a burner. Allow your guests to cook their lamb slices in the broth for a few minutes.

Your guests can customize their individual serving bowls with sauces, garnishes, etc. Place the cooked Lo Mein noodles in their bowls and ladle broth over the noodles. Enjoy.

9. Beef Noodle Soup

Delicious beef noodle soup recipe with noodles and spices!

Time: 2 - 8 hours

Servings: 8 - 10

Ingredients

Broth

- 5 lb. beef bones
- 1 inch piece rock sugar, + more to taste
- 1 tbsp salt, + more to taste
- 20 cups water
- 1 med yellow onion, peeled
- Chicken stock powder, to taste

Pho aroma

- Med yellow onion, unpeeled and halved

- Thumb-size knobs ginger, cut lengthwise into 1/8-inch-thick slices
- 3 star anise
- 2 cinnamon sticks
- 2 or 3 black cardamom pods
- 3 sprigs Asian basil
- 1 tsp cloves (optional)
- 1 tsp coriander seeds (optional)
- 3 1/3 lb. cooked Lo Mein noodles
- 10½ oz beef, thinly sliced
- 1 yellow onion, sliced thinly, soaked in ice water for 16 mins, drained
- 3-5 scallions (green parts chopped; white bits whole, smashed, blanched)

Directions:

For broth: put the beef bones in a pot filled with water that covers them. Bring to a boil cook for 5-10 mins, until all the impurities rise to the top. Drain the pot rinse the bones well under running water to wash away.

Place the bones in a pot the water. Add the onion, 1 tbsp. salt, and thumb-size piece rock sugar to the pot. Bring to boil, lower heat to low, simmer, uncovered. From time to time, skim off the scum.

For aroma: heat the onion 1/2s ginger slices directly on top of an open flame on the stove until a bit charred on all sides. Peel the onion carefully. Rinse the onion ginger under warm water remove off the charred.

Toast the cinnamon sticks, star anise, black cardamom pods, cloves (if using), coriander seeds (if using) in a pan on med-low heat until fragrant, about 2 mins. Place these spices in a spice ball/large tea/spice bag(s) or just wrap in a piece of cheesecloth. Add in the spices the charred onion ginger into the stockpot 30-45 mins before serving.

Place the thinly sliced beef onto a plate then add garnishes into bowls. Place your choice of dipping sauce on the table.

Pour broth into your Hotpot on the table, over a burner. Allow your guests to cook their beef slices in the broth for a few minutes.

Your guests can customize their individual serving bowls with sauces, garnishes, etc. Place the cooked Lo Mein noodles in their bowls and ladle broth over the noodles. Enjoy!

10. Lamb Noodle Hotpot Soup

Your guests will absolutely love this aromatic lamb soup!

Time: 2 - 8 hours

Servings: 8 - 10

Ingredients:

Broth

- 5 lb. lamb bones
- 1 inch piece rock sugar, + more to taste
- 1 tbsp salt, + more to taste
- 20 cups water
- 1 med yellow onion, peeled
- Chicken stock powder, to taste

Aroma

- Med yellow onion, unpeeled and halved
- Thumb-size knobs ginger, cut lengthwise into 1/8-inch-thick slices

- 3 star anise
- 2 cinnamon sticks
- 2 or 3 black cardamom pods
- 3 sprigs Asian basil
- 1 tsp cloves (optional)
- 1 tsp coriander seeds (optional)
- 3 1/3 lb. cooked Lo Mein noodles
- 10½ oz lamb, thinly sliced
- 1 yellow onion, sliced thinly, soaked in ice water for 16 mins, drained
- 3-5 scallions (green parts chopped; white bits whole, smashed, blanched)

Directions:

For broth: put the bones in a pot filled with water that covers them. Bring to a boil cook for 5-10 mins, until all the impurities rise to the top. Drain the pot rinse the bones well under running water to wash away.

Place the bones in a pot the water. Add the onion, 1 tbsp. salt, and thumb-size piece rock sugar to the pot. Bring to boil, lower heat to low, simmer, uncovered. From time to time, skim off the scum.

For aroma: heat the onion 1/2s ginger slices directly on top of an open flame on the stove until a bit charred on all sides. Peel the onion carefully. Rinse the onion ginger under warm water remove off the charred.

Toast the cinnamon sticks, star anise, black cardamom pods, cloves (if using), coriander seeds (if using) in a pan on med-low heat until fragrant, about 2 mins. Place these spices in a spice ball/large tea/spice bag(s) or just wrap in a piece of cheesecloth. Add in the spices the charred onion ginger into the stockpot 30-45 mins before serving.

Place the thinly sliced lamb onto a plate then add garnishes into bowls. Place your choice of dipping sauce on the table.

Pour broth into your Hotpot on the table, over a burner. Allow your guests to cook their lamb slices in the broth for a few minutes.

Your guests can customize their individual serving bowls with sauces, garnishes, etc. Place the cooked Lo Mein noodles in their bowls and ladle broth over the noodles. Enjoy!

11. Thai Shrimp Hotpot

Delicious shrimp Hotpot with Thai spices!

Time: 20 mins

Servings: 2

Ingredients:

- 10 oz. med-size shrimp, nicely peeled and deveined
- 3 tbsp fresh ginger, peeled and very thinly slivered
- 2 ½ tbsp fish sauce or soy sauce
- 3 carrots, thinly sliced
- 3 cups coarsely chopped fresh spinach
- 2 cloves garlic, finely minced
- 2 tsp chopped fresh basil
- 10 cups water
- 3 packets of chicken flavored Ramen noodles

- 4 green onions, minced
- 2 tbsp Thai hot chili sauce
- Juice and grated zest from 1 ½ limes
- 1 cup sliced mushrooms

Directions:

Fill a large pot with water. Bring this water to a boil on a high flame.

Add the carrots, fish sauce, green onions, ginger, garlic, basil and chili sauce.

Break the noodles and put them into the water as well. Keep stirring to separate the strands.

Now add the seasoning from 2 packets that came with the noodles. Boil for 5 minutes or so.

Pour broth into your Hotpot on the table, over a burner. Allow your guests to cook their shrimp, mushrooms and spinach in the broth for a few minutes.

Your guests can customize their individual serving bowls with sauces, garnishes, etc.

Enjoy!

12. Egg Noodle Hotpot

Delicious egg Hotpot with noodles, mushrooms and pork belly.

Time: 1hour

Serves: 4

Ingredients:

- 10 oz. pork belly
- ¼ cup dried wood fungus
- 8 dried shiitake mushrooms
- 2 tbsp peanut oil
- 1 tbsp fresh ginger, minced
- 3 spring onions, green part only, finely sliced
- ½ cup bamboo shoots, cut into matchsticks
- 4 cups chicken stock
- 1 tsp salt
- 2 tbsp soy sauce
- 1 tbsp shaohsing rice wine
- 11 oz. fresh flat egg noodles
- ½ cup ham, sliced into thin strips
- 1 tbsp cornstarch, combined with 1 tbsp water
- 2 eggs, beaten

- 1 tsp sesame oil
- ½ tsp pepper

Directions:

Put pork belly in a saucepan, cover with cold water and bring to the boil. Skim off any nasty stuff, reduce heat and simmer for 45 minutes. Turn off the heat and leave pork in the liquid to cool.

Soak the wood fungus and mushrooms separately in hot water for about an hour. Drain and rinse well, then cut into thin strips, discarding any stems.

Cut the cooled pork into thin strips about 1 in wide (reserve the cooking liquid, skimming off the fat).

Heat peanut oil in a saucepan. Then, cook ginger, mushrooms, wood fungus and bamboo shoots and stir fry briefly. Add chicken stock and 4 cups of the pork cooking liquid and bring to the boil. Add salt, soy sauce and rice wine, taste, adjust seasonings, and simmer for 3 minutes.

Cook noodles in boiling water for about a minute. Drain, rinse in cold water drain again. Return to the saucepan, off the heat, and keep warm.

Pour soup into your Hotpot on the table, over a burner. Allow your guests to put the pork, ham and eggs in the broth for a few minutes.

Your guests can customize their individual serving bowls with sauces, garnishes, etc.

Enjoy.

13. Ramen Shrimp Hotpot

A delicious ramen recipe with shrimps and carrots.

Time: 20 mins

Serves: 2

Ingredients:

- 9 cups water
- 3 ramen noodle packets
- 10 oz. med shrimp, frozen, cooked, peeled and deveined
- 2 tsp dark oriental sesame oil
- ½ tsp red pepper, crushed
- 1 cup scallions, chopped
- ½ cup carrots, grated

Directions:

Take a clean and dry pot and add the water to it. Bring this up to a boil.

Now break the blocks of noodles into 4 pieces each and add them to the pot.

Cook for around 5 minutes while constantly stirring. This will ensure that the strands separate from each other. Cook until the noodles are tender.

Transfer contents into your Hotpot on the table, over a burner. Allow your guests to add the shrimp and the packets of seasoning as well as the oil, scallions carrots and crushed peppers to the pot immediately.

Your guests can customize their individual serving bowls with sauces, garnishes, etc.

Enjoy!

14. Prawn and Noodle Hotpot

Prawns with noodles, veggies and mushrooms.

Time: 20 mins

Servings: 2

Ingredients:

- 3 tbsp fresh ginger, peeled and very thinly slivered
- 10 oz med-size prawns, nicely peeled and deveined
- 2 ½ tbsp fish sauce or soy sauce
- 3 carrots, thinly sliced
- 3 cups coarsely chopped fresh spinach
- 2 cloves garlic, finely minced
- 2 tsp fresh basil, chopped
- 10 cups water
- 3 packets of chicken flavored Ramen noodles
- 4 green onions, minced
- 2 tbsp Thai hot chili sauce

- Juice and grated zest from 1 ½ limes
- 1 cup sliced mushrooms

Directions:

Fill a large pot with water. Bring this water to a boil on a high flame.

Add the carrots, fish sauce, green onions, ginger, garlic, basil and chili sauce.

Break the noodles and put them into the water as well. Keep stirring to separate the strands.

Now add the seasoning from 2 packets that came with the noodles. Boil for 5 minutes or so.

Pour broth into your Hotpot on the table, over a burner. Allow your guests to cook their prawns, mushrooms and spinach in the broth for a few minutes.

Your guests can customize their individual serving bowls with sauces, garnishes, etc.

Enjoy!

15. Chicken Noodle Soup

Delicious chicken noodle soup recipe with spices!

Time: 2 - 8 hours

Makes: 8 - 10 servings

Ingredients

Broth

- 5 lb. chicken bones
- 1 inch piece rock sugar, + more to taste
- 1 tbsp salt, + more to taste
- 20 cups water
- 1 med yellow onion, peeled
- Chicken stock powder, to taste

Pho aroma

- Med yellow onion, unpeeled and halved
- Thumb-size knobs ginger, cut lengthwise into 1/8-inch-thick slices

- 3 star anise
- 2 cinnamon sticks
- 2 or 3 black cardamom pods
- 3 sprigs Asian basil
- 1 tsp cloves (optional)
- 1 tsp coriander seeds (optional)
- 3 1/3 lb. cooked Lo Mein noodles
- 10½ oz chicken breasts, thinly sliced
- 1 yellow onion, sliced thinly, soaked in ice water for 16 mins, drained
- 3-5 scallions (green parts chopped; white bits whole, smashed, blanched)

Directions:

For broth: put the bones in a pot filled with water that covers them. Bring to a boil cook for 5-10 mins, until all the impurities rise to the top. Drain the pot rinse the bones well under running water to wash away.

Place the bones in a pot the water. Add the onion, 1 tbsp. salt, and thumb-size piece rock sugar to the pot. Bring to boil, lower heat to low, simmer, uncovered. From time to time, skim off the scum.

For aroma: heat the onion 1/2s ginger slices directly on top of an open flame on the stove until a bit charred on all sides. Peel the onion carefully. Rinse the onion ginger under warm water remove off the charred.

Toast the cinnamon sticks, star anise, black cardamom pods, cloves (if using), coriander seeds (if using) in a pan on med-low heat until fragrant, about 2 mins. Place these spices in a spice ball/large tea/spice bag(s) or just wrap in a piece of cheesecloth. Add in the spices the charred onion ginger into the stockpot 30-45 mins before serving.

Place the thinly sliced chicken onto a plate then add garnishes into bowls. Place your choice of dipping sauce on the table.

Pour broth into your Hotpot on the table, over a burner. Allow your guests to cook their chicken slices in the broth for a few minutes.

Your guests can customize their individual serving bowls with sauces, garnishes, etc. Place the cooked Lo Mein noodles in their bowls and ladle broth over the noodles. Enjoy!

16. Duck Noodle Soup

A variation on the chicken noodle soup but with succulent duck instead!

Time: 2 - 8 hours

Makes: 8 - 10 servings

Ingredients

Broth

- 5 lb. duck bones
- 1 inch piece rock sugar, + more to taste
- 1 tbsp salt, + more to taste
- 20 cups water
- 1 med yellow onion, peeled
- Chicken stock powder, to taste

Pho aroma

- Med yellow onion, unpeeled and halved
- Thumb-size knobs ginger, cut lengthwise into 1/8-inch-thick slices

- 3 star anise
- 2 cinnamon sticks
- 2 or 3 black cardamom pods
- 3 sprigs Asian basil
- 1 tsp cloves (optional)
- 1 tsp coriander seeds (optional)
- 3 1/3 lb. cooked Lo Mein noodles
- 10½ oz duck breasts, thinly sliced
- 1 yellow onion, sliced thinly, soaked in ice water for 16 mins, drained
- 3-5 scallions (green parts chopped; white bits whole, smashed, blanched)

Directions:

For broth: put the bones in a pot filled with water that covers them. Bring to a boil cook for 5-10 mins, until all the impurities rise to the top. Drain the pot rinse the bones well under running water to wash away.

Place the bones in a pot the water. Add the onion, 1 tbsp. salt, and thumb-size piece rock sugar to the pot. Bring to boil, lower heat to low, simmer, uncovered. From time to time, skim off the scum.

For aroma: heat the onion 1/2s ginger slices directly on top of an open flame on the stove until a bit charred on all sides. Peel the onion carefully. Rinse the onion ginger under warm water remove off the charred.

Toast the cinnamon sticks, star anise, black cardamom pods, cloves (if using), coriander seeds (if using) in a pan on med-low heat until fragrant, about 2 mins. Place these spices in a spice ball/large tea/spice bag(s) or just wrap in a piece of cheesecloth. Add in the spices the charred onion ginger into the stockpot 30-45 mins before serving.

Place the thinly sliced chicken onto a plate then add garnishes into bowls. Place your choice of dipping sauce on the table.

Pour broth into your Hotpot on the table, over a burner. Allow your guests to cook their duck slices in the broth for a few minutes.

Your guests can customize their individual serving bowls with sauces, garnishes, etc. Place the cooked Lo Mein noodles in their bowls and ladle broth over the noodles. Enjoy!

17. Ramen Chicken Hotpot

A delicious ramen recipe with chicken, sesame oil and carrots.

Time: 20 mins

Serves: 2

Ingredients:

- 9 cups water
- 3 ramen noodle packets
- 10 oz chicken breasts, sliced and cooked
- 2 tsp dark oriental sesame oil
- ½ tsp crushed red pepper.
- 1 cup scallions, chopped
- ½ cup carrots, grated

Directions:

Take a clean and dry pot and add the water to it. Bring this up to a boil.

Now break the blocks of noodles into 4 pieces each and add them to the pot.

Cook for around 5 minutes while constantly stirring. This will ensure that the strands separate from each other. Cook until the noodles are tender.

Transfer contents into your Hotpot on the table, over a burner. Allow your guests to add the chicken and the packets of seasoning as well as the oil, scallion, carrots and crushed peppers to the pot immediately.

Your guests can customize their individual serving bowls with sauces, garnishes, etc.

Enjoy!

18. Chicken Ramen Soup

A hearty, comforting chicken noodle soup with peas and carrots.

Time: 15 mins

Serves: 4

Ingredients:

- 5 cups water
- 2 packets ramen noodles, chicken flavor
- 2 cups snow peas, sliced diagonally
- 2 green onions, sliced
- 1 large carrot, shredded
- 1 pound chicken breast
- 1 tsp Asian sesame oil

Directions:

Heat the water in a large saucepan and add the ramen seasoning packets.

Cut the chicken into bite-size pieces. Break up the ramen noodles into 2 layers.

Once the water and the seasoning have boiled, add the noodles, chicken, carrot, green onions, and snow peas. Cook over high for about 5 mins. Transfer contents into your Hotpot on the table, over a burner.

Your guests can customize their individual serving bowls with sauces, garnishes, etc.

Enjoy!

19. Spicy Beef and Mushroom Stew

This hearty, beefy stew has an addictively spicy edge, thanks to the ramen seasoning packet.

Time: 30 mins

Serves: 4

Ingredients:

- 4 teaspoons extra-virgin olive oil

- 1 onion, cut in half and sliced
- 2 rib celery, thinly sliced
- 2 carrots, peeled, halved lengthwise, thinly sliced
- 2 cups quartered cremini or white mushrooms
- 12 oz flank steak or hanger steak, cut into bite-size pieces
- 2 tablespoons balsamic vinegar
- 2 cups beef stock or broth
- 2 cups water
- 2 packages ramen noodles, chili flavor

Directions:

Heat the oil in a saucepan. Add the onion, celery, and carrot and sauté, stirring occasionally, until the vegetables are softened, about 5 minutes. Add the mushrooms and steak and sauté, stirring, until the steak is browned and the mushrooms are soft, 2 to 3 minutes. Add the wine and sauté, scraping the browned bits off the bottom of the pan, until most of the liquid has evaporated, 1-2 mins.

Add the stock or broth, water, and ramen seasoning. When simmering, reduce heat to low then cook for 10 minutes. Transfer contents into your Hotpot on the table, over a burner. Allow your guests to add the noodles and cook for a few minutes.

Your guests can customize their individual serving bowls with sauces, garnishes, etc.

Enjoy!

20. Lamb Pea Soup

Lamb, noodles, peas and carrots make up this aromatic soup.

Time: 15 mins

Serves: 4

Ingredients:

- 5 cups water
- 2 packets ramen noodles, chicken flavor
- 2 cups snow peas, sliced diagonally
- 2 green onions, sliced
- 1 large carrot, shredded
- 1 pound lamb flank, sliced into thin strips
- 1 tsp. Asian sesame oil

Directions:

Heat the water in a large saucepan and add the ramen seasoning packets.

Cut the chicken into bite-size pieces. Break up the ramen noodles into 2 layers.

Once the water and the seasoning have boiled, add the noodles, carrot, green onions, and snow peas. Cook over high for about 5 mins. Transfer contents into your Hotpot on the table, over a burner.

Allow your guests to cook their lamb in the Hotpot.

Your guests can customize their individual serving bowls with sauces, garnishes, etc.

Enjoy!

21. Tofu Pea Soup

Delicious tofu and pea soup with ramen.

Time: 15 mins

Serves: 4

Ingredients:

- 5 cups water
- 2 packets ramen noodles, vegetable flavor
- 2 cups snow peas, sliced diagonally
- 2 green onions, sliced
- 1 large carrot, shredded
- ½ lb. tofu, broken into pieces
- 1 tsp. Asian sesame oil

Directions:

Heat the water in a large saucepan and add the ramen seasoning packets.

Break up the ramen noodles into 2 layers.

Once the water and the seasoning have boiled, add the noodles, carrot, green onions, and snow peas. Cook on high heat for about 5 mins. Transfer contents into your hot pot on the table, over a burner.

Allow your guests to cook their tofu in the hot pot.

Your guests can customize their individual serving bowls with sauces, garnishes, etc.

Enjoy!

22. Beef Ramen Soup with Veggies

Beef and ramen with carrots and snow peas.

Time: 15 mins

Serves: 4

Ingredients:

- 5 cups water
- 2 packets ramen noodles, chicken flavor
- 2 cups snow peas, sliced diagonally
- 2 green onions, sliced
- 1 large carrot, shredded
- 1 pound beef, sliced into thin strips
- 1 tsp Asian sesame oil

Directions:

Heat the water in a large saucepan and add the ramen seasoning packets.

Cut the chicken into bite size pieces. Break up the ramen noodles into 2 layers.

Once the water and the seasoning have boiled, add the noodles, carrot, green onions, and snow peas. Cook on high heat for about 5 mins. Transfer contents into your Hotpot on the table, over a burner.

Allow your guests to cook their beef in the Hotpot.

Your guests can customize their individual serving bowls with sauces, garnishes, etc.

Enjoy!

23. Cauliflower Pea Soup

A delicious veggie option for people who don't eat meat!

Time: 15 mins

Serves: 4

Ingredients:

- 5 cups water
- 2 packets ramen noodles, vegetable flavor
- 2 cups snow peas, sliced diagonally
- 2 green onions, sliced
- 1 large carrot, shredded
- 1 pound cauliflower, chopped
- 1 tsp Asian sesame oil

Directions:

Heat the water in a large saucepan and add the ramen seasoning packets.

Break up the ramen noodles into 2 layers.

Once the water and the seasoning have boiled, add the noodles, carrot, green onions, and snow peas. Cook on high heat for about 5 mins. Transfer contents into your Hotpot on the table, over a burner.

Allow your guests to cook their cauliflower in the Hotpot.

Your guests can customize their individual serving bowls with sauces, garnishes, etc.

Enjoy!

24. Chicken Lemongrass Soup

Thai flavors combined with chicken and lemongrass soup.

Time: 15 mins

Serves: 4

Ingredients:

For the seasoning sauce:

- 3 tbsp fresh lime juice
- 2 tbsp fish sauce
- 2 tbsp Thai Chili Paste or more to taste
- 1/2 tsp salt

For the soup:

- 4 cups (1 liter) water or chicken stock

- Six 1/8-in (3-mm) thick slices galangal (Thai ginger)
- 2 kaffir lime leaves, torn into small bits
- 1 stalk lemongrass, crushed and cut into 2-in (5-cm) lengths
- 1 lb. (500 g) boneless, skinless chicken breast, sliced into 2 x 1 x 1/8-inch pieces
- 1 cup (100 g) fresh mushrooms, thinly sliced
- 2 cherry tomatoes, halved
- 1 green onion (scallion), finely chopped
- 1 stem fresh coriander, finely chopped

Directions:

In a small bowl, combine together all the seasoning sauce and set aside.

Heat the water or stock in a large saucepan over high heat until it boils. Add in the galangal, lime leaves, and lemongrass. Cook for 2 to 3 minutes to allow the flavors to intensify. Remove the herbs with a slotted spoon. Then, discard them.

Transfer contents into your Hotpot on the table, over a burner.

Allow your guests to cook their chicken meat, mushrooms and tomatoes in the Hotpot for a few minutes. They can then add in the seasoning sauce, green onion and fresh coriander.

Enjoy!

25. Mushroom Soup

Mushroom soup with ramen, red chili sauce and sesame oil.

Time: 15 mins

Serves: 4

Ingredients:

- 5 cups water
- 2 packets ramen noodles, vegetable flavor
- 2 cups snow peas, sliced diagonally
- 2 green onions, sliced
- 1 large carrot, shredded
- 1 pound mushrooms, chopped
- 1 tsp Asian sesame oil
- 1 tsp red chili sauce

Directions:

Heat the water in a large saucepan and add the ramen seasoning packets.

Break up the ramen noodles into 2 layers.

Once the water and the seasoning have boiled, add the noodles, carrot, green onions, and snow peas, and oil and sauce. Cook on high heat for about 5 mins. Transfer contents into your Hotpot on the table, over a burner.

Allow your guests to cook their mushrooms in the Hotpot.

Your guests can customize their individual serving bowls with sauces, garnishes, etc.

Enjoy!

26. Thai Mushroom Hotpot

A delicious Hotpot experience with mushroom and Thai spices.

Time: 30 mins

Servings: 10

Ingredients:

- 2 tbsp fresh Lime juice
- 1 tbsp Garlic powder
- 1 tsp ground Ginger
- 2 tbsp low sodium Soy sauce
- 1 tbsp brown Sugar, lightly packed
- 2 tsp Vegetable oil
- 1 Sweet onion, thinly sliced, large

- 2 (32 oz) Containers of beef stock
- 1/4 cup, red Curry paste
- 1 lb. Mushrooms, thinly sliced

Sauces

- Tangy chili sauce
- Dipping sauce that you desire
- Cooked Lo Mein Noodles

Directions:

To create a broth, heat the oil into a large stock pot over medium-high heat. Add the onion then stir to combine, cook until tender.

Stir while you add garlic powder, ginger, soy sauce, brown sugar, curry paste, and stock. Bring to boil then lower heat. Cover pan. Simmer for 20 mins then mix in the lime juice into the broth.

Place the thinly sliced steak onto a plate then add garnishes into bowls. Place your choice of dipping sauce on the table.

Pour broth into your Hotpot on the table, over a burner. Allow your guests to cook their mushrooms in the broth for a few minutes.

Your guests can customize their individual serving bowls with sauces, garnishes, etc. Place the cooked Lo Mein noodles in their bowls and ladle broth over the noodles. Enjoy.

27. Chicken Curry Udon Hotpot

A delicious Japanese curry recipe with udon noodles.

Time: 20mins

Serves: 4

Ingredients:

- 10 oz dried udon
- 2 tbsp peanut oil
- 2 onions, sliced
- 11 oz boned, chicken thigh, cut into bite-size cubes
- 1 cup green beans, blanched
- 2 tsp curry powder
- 4 cups chicken stock
- 1 tsp sugar
- 2 tbsp tapioca starch or potato starch

- 2 spring onions, finely sliced

Directions:

Boil water and add noodles. When water turns to the boil, add 1 cup cold water. When water again returns to the boil, add another cup cold water. Repeat the process another 2 to 4 times, depending on thickness of udon, until the noodles are cooked but still have a little resilience. Drain, rinse in cold water and set aside.

Heat oil and fry onion gently for a couple of minutes. Add beans and cook for 1 minute. Sprinkle on curry powder and mix in with a wooden spoon. Pour in stock and sugar, bring to the boil and simmer for 3 minutes. Mix tapioca starch with a little water. Pour contents into your Hotpot on the table, over a burner. Allow your guests to cook their chicken bites in the sauce for a few minutes.

Your guests can customize their individual serving bowls with sauces, garnishes, etc. Place the cooked noodles in their bowls and ladle sauce over the noodles. Enjoy.

28. Penang laksa

When most people think of laksa, they think of curry laksa, or laksa lemak. But the people of Penang have devised their own laksa using fish. Rather than thick, creamy and coconutty, this laksa is sour and brothy – a totally different kettle of fish.

Time: 20mins

Serves: 4

Ingredients:

- 4 cups cold water
- ½ tsp salt
- 1 lb. blue mackerel, or other firm-fleshed fish
- 2 cups tamarind water
- 2 stalks of lemongrass, white part only, finely sliced
- 2 tsp ground turmeric
- 1 tbsp belacan (shrimp paste)
- 6 dried chilies, soaked, drained and chopped
- ¾ inch piece galangal or ginger, finely chopped
- 1 tbsp palm sugar, or white sugar
- 10 oz round rice noodles or Hokkien noodles

- 1 cucumber, peeled, cut into thin matchsticks

Directions:

Bring water and salt to the boil, add fish and simmer for 5 minutes. Remove fish, cool, then flake off flesh with your hands and set aside. Return heads and bones to the water. Add tamarind water and simmer for a further 10 minutes, then strain through a fine sieve and set stock aside.

Pound or blend lemongrass, turmeric, belacan, chili and galangal to a paste. Add to fish stock with sugar and simmer for 10 minutes.

Pour contents into your hot pot on the table, over a burner. Allow your guests to add the fish in to heat it through.

Your guests can customize their individual serving bowls with sauces, garnishes, etc. Place the cooked noodles in their bowls and ladle broth over the noodles.

Enjoy!

29. Japanese Veggie Curry

Veggies in Japanese-flavoured curry. Simple and delicious!

Time: 20mins

Serves: 4

Ingredients:

- 10 oz dried udon
- 2 tbsp peanut oil
- 2 onions, sliced
- 4 cups mushrooms, sliced
- 1 cup green beans, blanched
- 2 tsp curry powder
- 4 cups chicken stock
- 1 tsp sugar
- 2 tbsp tapioca starch or potato starch

- 2 spring onions, finely sliced

Directions:

Boil water and add noodles. When water turns to the boil, add 1 cup cold water. When water again returns to the boil, add another cup cold water. Repeat the process another 2 to 4 times, depending on thickness of udon, until the noodles are cooked but still have a little resilience. Drain, rinse in cold water and set aside.

Heat oil and fry onion gently for a couple of minutes. Add beans and cook for 1 minute. Sprinkle on curry powder and mix in with a wooden spoon. Pour in stock and sugar, bring to the boil and simmer for 3 minutes. Mix tapioca starch with a little water. Pour contents into your Hotpot on the table, over a burner. Allow your guests to cook their mushroom in the sauce for a few minutes.

Your guests can customize their individual serving bowls with sauces, garnishes, etc. Place the cooked noodles in their bowls and ladle sauce over the noodles. Enjoy.

30. Tofu Lemongrass Soup

This delicious recipe with tofu and lemongrass is perfect for people who don't eat meat!

Time: 15 mins

Serves: 4

Ingredients:

For the seasoning sauce:

- 3 tbsp. fresh lime juice
- 2 tbsp. fish sauce
- 2 tbsp. Thai Chili Paste or more to taste
- 1/2 tsp. salt

For the soup:

- 4 cups (1 liter) water or veggie stock
- Six 1/8-in (3-mm) thick slices galangal (Thai ginger)
- 2 kaffir lime leaves, torn into small bits

- 3 cups firm tofu
- 1 stalk lemongrass, crushed and cut into 2-in (5-cm) lengths
- 1 cup (100 g) thinly sliced fresh mushrooms
- 2 cherry tomatoes, halved
- 1 green onion (scallion), finely chopped
- 1 stem fresh coriander, finely chopped

Directions:

In a small bowl, combine together all the seasoning sauce and set aside.

Heat the water or stock in a large saucepan over high heat until it boils. Add in the galangal, lime leaves, and lemongrass. Cook for 2 to 3 minutes to allow the flavors to intensify. Remove the herbs with a slotted spoon and discard them.

Transfer contents into your Hotpot on the table, over a burner.

Allow your guests to cook their tofu, mushrooms and tomatoes in the Hotpot for a few minutes. They can then add in the seasoning sauce, green onion and fresh coriander.

Enjoy!

Conclusion

Well, there you have it folks! 30 delicious, appetizing and flavorful recipes for you and your guests to enjoy in a Hotpot. Be sure to try out all the recipes and remember to share them with your friends and family!

Author's Afterthoughts

Thank you for Purchasing my book and taking the time to read it from front to back. I am always grateful when a reader chooses my work and I hope you enjoyed it!

With the vast selection available online, I am touched that you chose to be purchasing my work and take valuable time out of your life to read it. My hope is that you feel you made the right decision.

Printed in Great Britain
by Amazon